LEARNING TO SOLVE PROBLEMS WITH TECHNOLOGY

A Constructivist Perspective

Second Edition

David H. Jonassen
University of Missouri

Jane Howland
University of Missouri

Joi Moore
University of Missouri

Rose M. Marra
University of Missouri

Merrill
Prentice Hall

Upper Saddle River, New Jersey
Columbus, Ohio

Library of Congress Cataloging in Publication Data

Learning to solve problems with technology: a constructivist perspective/David H. Jonassen . . . [et al.].
    p. cm.
  Rev. ed. of: Learning with technology. c1999.
  Includes bibliographical references and index.
   1. Educational technology. 2. Teaching—Aids and devices. 3. Learning. 4. Constructivism (Education) I. Jonassen, David H., II. Jonassen, David H., Learning with technology.

LB1028.3 .J63 2003
371.33—dc21

2002070985

Vice President and Publisher: Jeffery W. Johnston
Executive Editor: Debra A. Stollenwerk
Editorial Assistant: Mary Morrill
Production Editor: JoEllen Gohr
Production Coordination: Clarinda Publication Services
Photo Coordinator: Cynthia Cassidy
Design Coordinator: Diane C. Lorenzo
Cover Designer: Thomas Borah
Cover Photo: Image Bank
Production Manager: Pamela Bennett
Director of Marketing: Ann Castel Davis
Marketing Manager: Krista Groshong
Marketing Coordinator: Tyra Cooper

This book was set in Palatino by The Clarinda Company.
The cover was printed by Phoenix Color Corp.

Photo Credits: p. 1, SW Productions, Getty Images, Inc./PhotoDisc, Inc.; p. 19, David Buffington, Getty Images, Inc./PhotoDisc, Inc.; pp. 31, 209, Anthony Magnacca/Merrill; pp. 69, 121, 134, 163, Scott Cunningham/Merrill; p. 189, University of Washington HIT Lab/Mary Levin; p. 227, Anne Vega/Merrill. All other photos supplied by the authors.

Pearson Education Ltd.
Pearson Education Australia Pty. Limited
Pearson Education Singapore Ptc. Ltd.
Pearson Education North Asia Ltd.
Pearson Education, Canada, Ltd.
Pearson Educación de Mexico, S.A. de C.V.
Pearson Education—Japan
Pearson Education Malaysia Pte, Ltd.
Pearson Education, *Upper Saddle River, New Jersey*

1 0 9 8 7 6
ISBN 0-13-048403-2